T0197404

Unyielding Circumstances of Chronicles Undefined

DR. OCTAVIA KINCY-MOTEN

AuthorHouse™
1663 Liberty Drive
Bloomington, IN 47403
www.authorhouse.com
Phone: 833-262-8899

Scripture quotations marked KJV are from the Holy Bible, King James Version (Authorized Version). First published
in 1611. Quoted from the KJV Classic Reference Bible, Copyright © 1983 by The Zondervan Corporation.

ISBN: 978-1-6655-2932-7 (sc)
ISBN: 978-1-6655-2934-1 (hc)
ISBN: 978-1-6655-2933-4 (e)

Print information available on the last page.

Published by AuthorHouse 06/28/2021

author HOUSE®

Table of Contents

Unyielding Circumstances of Chronicles Undefined

Unyielding = Hard

Circumstances = State of Affairs in One's Life

of

Chronicles = *History

Undefined = Forever

ONLY ANSWER = HOLY SPIRIT

John 14:26 (King James Version)

But the Comforter, which is the **Holy** Ghost, whom the Father will send in my name, he shall teach you all things, and bring all things to your remembrance, whatsoever I have said unto you.

I. The Road Less Traveled

With twists and turns unraveling once more,
We've traveled this road far too many times before.

It's a repeated cycle of unwanted faithful bliss.
At which end of ceasing is this twist?

One, two, three, and then four—
Life ensues purpose beyond this door.

Limitless counting towards that which lies ahead:
Bountiful endeavors from which our ancestors dread.

Being a vessel once again, we trod
Galloping and panting in the direction called fraud.

A cornucopia of truth has been bestowed upon us once more.
Truth, faith, and life knocking at Heaven's door.

II. To Him Who Is Faithful

Circumstance and virtue cross our daily path,
For whence came ignorance according to *him* who hath:

Destiny and survival among the fittest constitute longsuffering to say at its best.
Being faithful is the first act of godliness.

"Say what you want, and do as you will!"
Triggering justice at the footholds for all men is not what most of us feel.

Justifying wrongdoings behooves the walking dead among us.
Remaining silent is no longer but now creating all the fuss.

Trust not the system to correct sins of our past,
For justice will finally be ours at last!

Do not contemplate the time that it takes to fix what's not right,

But keep the faith in Him with all our might!

III. Chronicles of Man's Journey Undefined

Our hearts are heavy yet filled with grief.
How long is the suffering for this unbelief?

Various perceptions of both genders but yet alike
Are similar to the contrite feelings of those who attempt this plight.

A man's journey is never complete
According to the riches and glory bestowed upon others' feet.

The definition journeyed has no definition or intention of being defined
Unyielding circumstances of chronicles undefined!

See page 1

IV. *Mystery, Murder, and Mischief*

All caused our family such horrible pain and grief!

Material items were lost and will not be restored,
But for all of us who are Christians know He has the final say to those who adored:

The life taken earlier than originally planned
Has to be accounted for in the Master's plan.

Lest not focus our energy on what should or should not have taken place,
For in the end, justice is not ours to decide this case.

We are to carry on and move forward with life,
And be obedient servants and trust God's timing with the sins of others who might:

Be guilty of a crime committed through
Mystery,
Murder, and
Mischief.

God is the
Judge,
Juror,
Jury, and
Ultimate Chief!

Emphasis on Chief,
The only One to judge this
Mischief.

As a reminder:
The guilty was never the *chief*!

The guilty was and will forever be only "blood relation" who committed
Mystery,
Murder, and
Mischief!

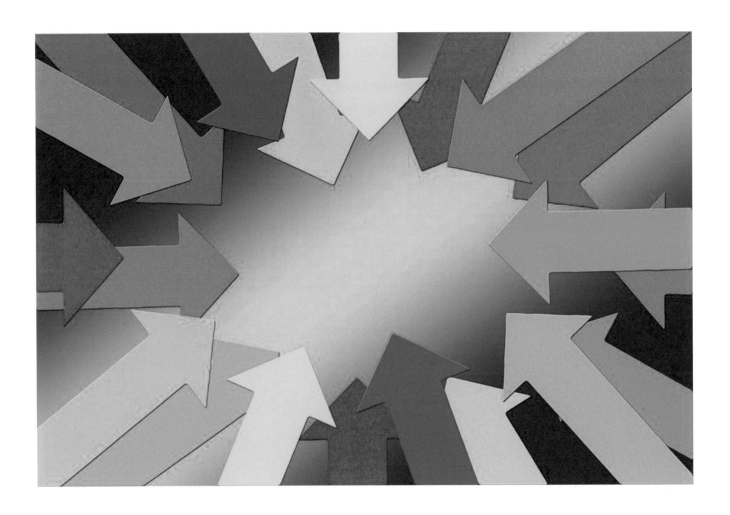

V. Rescued Midstream

In the middle of this captivating and cultivating dream—
Through the parables from afar to capture devastation but yet self-esteem.

For by his submission, one's own defeat is proclaimed.
From whence His assurance be it disdained.

Rightfully yet tactfully so is the course from this fight or flight—
With all of His strength and enduring might.

Created from above, His abundance is pure joy—
Misleading never but overpowered by removing alloy.

To offer reassurance for what's cometh ahead: constant reminders of His joy *personified*—
His will and grace, He always provides!

Through the middle of this pandemic, His faith is restored!
Trusting in Him three times over constitutes a reassured rescue by His hands adored!

And He ˢrules over the ⁿⁿⁿⁿⁿ
29 All the ᵇprosperous of the earth will eat ᵃⁿⁿ ⁿⁿⁿ
All those who ᵍgo down to the dust will ⁿⁿⁿ
Him,
Even he who ᵇcannot keep his soul alive.
30 ᵃPosterity will serve Him;
It will be told of the Lord to ᵇthe coming generation.
31 They will come and ᵃwill declare His righteousness
To a people ᵇwho will be born, that He has performed

PSALM 23

The LORD, the Psalmist's Shepherd.
A Psalm of David.

1 The LORD is my ᵃshepherd,
  I ¹shall ᵇnot want.
2 He makes me lie down in ᵃgreen pastures;
  He ᵇleads me beside ¹ᶜquiet waters.
3 He ᵃrestores my soul;
  He ᵇguides me in the ¹ᶜpaths of righteousness
For His name's sake.

4 Even though I ᵃwalk through the ¹valley of the sh

VI. *Faithfulness Restored*

Upon others dismayed,
His strength and wisdom shall conquer today.

Amongst us, whom shall we fear?
The man in the mirror for whom we shall cheer.

Stress, strife, struggles abundantly unwound
Challenging our heartstrings abound.

His principles aloft our treacherous past
Seemingly knowing ours would not last.

He's the *Almighty King in light and dark*
Restoring our entire existence however embark.

We always consistently and constantly inquire, "How do we arrive there?"
Patience is a virtue is what we were told from *angels* unaware.

Restore our faith, that mustard seed in the flesh.
Surely *His goodness and mercy* chose us at *His best*.

We're *His offspring* attempting to reach the fold.
He is our everlasting and glistening gold.

Faith in abundance has been restored!
"Count your blessings forever and again once more!"

VII. Lessons Learned

The feeling of having been ostracized from what seems real but known as **_our past_**
Does not define who we are but creates a new self-identity loaded with aghast.

Those who are distant exist there for a reason.
Time being of an essence has denoted this treason.

Faithlessness is what we have found in foes.
Faithfulness has ended all those woes.

Since our feet are now planted toward future lessons to grasp,
There's only one solution for attainment, and that's with a stronghold clasp.

The past can be a deterrent or reflection sometimes, even often blurred,
But direction and peace are found only in _His_ Word.

From past lessons, reminiscing was not at all times organically peaceful—
Yes, and no, but the message, good or bad was consistently meaningful.

One of the most difficult concepts to accept throughout life comes from _His_ Word,
And that is _His_ message regarding death which has been conferred.

"And God shall wipe away all tears from their eyes;
and there shall be no more death,
neither sorrow, nor crying,
neither shall there be any more pain:
for the former things are passed away."

King James Version (Revelation 21:4)

VIII. In the Beginning

Before the womb, there was no way of knowing what God already knew:
That life is predestined as His plan through and through!

He created our life as a plan unfold,
A vision with purpose contrary to what others uphold.

All that prejudging, judgment, and trials in others' mind—
Do not pay attention to anything unless it's through His will and aligned!

Search and search but look no further.
Enter and remain in this life as a precursor to being only an observer.

Observe His goodness, greatness, and favor alike.
Our prelude, beginning, & end are testaments: images in His likeness, what we should be like!

You are your biggest obstacle!

IX. Being Far Is Not Being Last

Perhaps, this could appear as a misconception, but its meaning remains the same.
Our mind, as well as our thinking can be transformed by the help of only one name:

Our Savior lives within us, but unbeknownst for others, they choose to think and live alone.
Although possible, all of us could be far from the truth or destination unknown.

Does being far mean being last in any sense of the word?
A long-term goal could be far, still within reach, but never unattainable or unheard.

A far-reaching goal would never surmount to being the last goal achievable.
Far or last is just a mindset and perhaps an unmentionable.

We should ask ourselves, "How far am I from finishing or winning?"
"Last place—that's absurd because our mind should always take us to the beginning:

Of knowing: *'I'm not just trying to be a winner. I'm always a winner at this thing called life!'*
Being far is not being last; far is never last. <u>It's that internal struggle creating constant strife</u>."

X. Forgive and Forget

Total forgiveness is forgetting altogether!
There would not be a reason to rehash it—never.

Forgiving others is wholly liberating our soul
And simultaneously relinquishing total control.

It's damaging for our inner being to hold on and not forgive.
Forgive and forget is a surefire way to successfully live!

We often say, "I will forgive you, but I won't forget."
How contradictory— let bygones be bygones and release that regret!

XI. Leading Despite Temptation

Born leaders would not succumb to temptation
But would release their innate talents to strengthen locally and globally beyond our nation.

Choosing life beyond temptation is challenging within itself, but leading despite is another!
Inadvertently, execution of strong leadership qualities is oftentimes inherited from our mother.

Temptation is also powerful, but a true leader by nature cannot be tempted
Whether the leadership is by nature or nurture preempted.

Lead with love and integrity alike—
Trials and temptation despite!

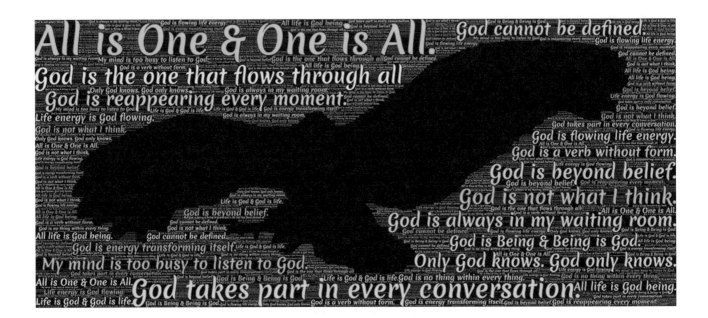

XII. Mind Over Matter

Mind over matter is a concept of infusion heightened by more than an illusion.
His Word speaks against being double-minded which is merely confusion.

According to His Word, a double-minded man is unstable in all of his ways.
A strong-willed mind can conquer the world throughout his days.

Mind over matter is how we should eternally live our life.
Without our Savior, matter over mind would cause unnecessary strife.

XIII. Take Time to Study

God has granted us with many gifts and talents, especially when studying the field of our choice.
In dreams, goals, hopes, visions, and wishes, His Word: first and only option to uplift His voice.

Studying His Word as a means of being an only way out—
Choosing and making the field of our desire about/with Him, when in doubt.

Also, He will grant us the desires of our heart.
Taking time to study His Word is doing our part!

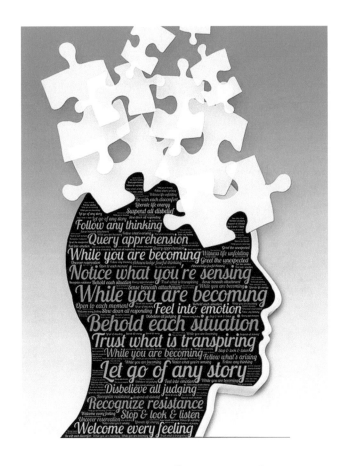

XIV. Within Reach

All things are possible and within reach of our realm!
With God as Captain, He is Head of the helm.

Blessings, boundaries, dreams, fruitions, goals, and testimonies are all limitless.
With the Holy Spirit in charge, our only operative action is to progress.

We are to scream and shout from every hilltop or highest mountain abound
Proclaiming that His reach is nothing short of being profound!

XV. Should I or Shouldn't I?

If we repeatedly inquire, then the answer is, "No."
Listening to the heart is a confirmation of *go*.

Reliving or revisiting, especially if it's almost nightmarish and haunting suggest should *not*.
Our gut feeling is more than innate or instinctive but a *sure shot*.

If our answer is provided from the heavens above without a shadow of doubt,
There's no need to question when our innate instinctive confirmation is divinely devout.

XVI. The Confirmation

Praying for an answer is the surest way from whence our help cometh.

The measures by which we took define our individual take on the doeth.

Confirmation comes from people, places, and things to say the least unexpecteth,

But trust and believe God delivers confirmation by any means showing signs that are assureth.

His Word is the Foundation for which we shall seeketh.

His confirmation cometh through those who pray, trust, and believeth!

XVII. When We Have Nothing

Let us erase from our minds all materialistic values of nothingness.
Our society has made any and every thing materialistic noteworthy of being success.

Nothing could be an answer, gesture, sentence, thought, or word that we cannot communicate.
If we ask God for any and all that we seek, His miracles He would make available to articulate.

Nothing is the opposite of which our Shepherd provides for His sheep.
Prayerfully, all things, anything, and everything constitute being in His Word at knee-deep.

XVIII. PRAY ALL DAY

Prayer is a privilege and right because we are free.
Our devoted effort and time could last for eternity.

Prayer is an act of a righteous man.
No pun intended for yet the gender undefined is a part of *His plan*.

It's up to us if we exercise this right knowing that prayers are already answered.
It's our acceptance of *His answer* that we do not wish to accept, oftentimes, the unanswered.

It may or may not be that which goes in our favor.
Just know *His goodness* is never an option or right that's a waiver.

Praying is an act that should be practiced every day and all day.
He has shown us time and time again that *prayer* is the only way!

Throughout every blessed hour—hour after hour,
For *He* listens because *prayer* is our very own superpower!

XIX. Time

When does the madness stop? Will it ever end?
How do we sincerely view life itself? Or shall we continue to pretend?

We cannot pinpoint when it actually started,
but in all fairness, *time is of the essence* or perhaps thwarted.

We should allow God to be the Messenger within us who shines.
Henceforth, we will never again question madness or existence of times.

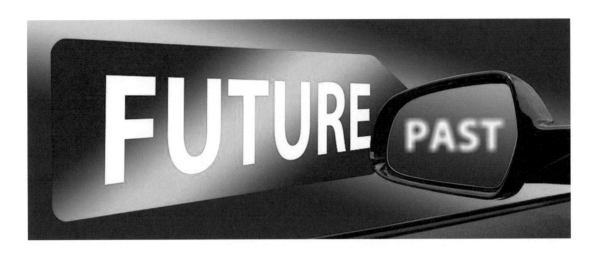

XX. Different from the Rest
Yet for some, may be considered the best.

Best by far is next to none.
Who is the Decider and will answer, "Who won?"

We should only and always listen to the One,
Our Lord and Savior, the chosen One for some.

It will be a glorious day on Earth when He is accepted by all!
Until then, praying night and day is a must for Him to catch us all when we fall.

It's our duty and nothing less
For us proclaiming to the world that He is our best!

The best by far, He is Truth—Light,
A beacon of light for darkness— His strength and might!

When we build or strengthen that personal relationship with God,
No weapon formed against us shall prosper in His eyes—a life and future unflawed!

XXI. JUST ASK

Today is not ours to perfectly claim,
But we could not reframe it by any other name.

Though, we will seek or continue to find
Life more abundantly ours, yours, and mine.

His assistance never ceases.
Without Him, there is no picking up the pieces.

He casts, gives, grants, or provides everything in full and threefold.
We're the ones not asking or standing on faith throughout all strongholds.

XXII. TEACH US HOW

Teach us. Show us. Tell us *what* to do.
Our burning desire is learning *how* we get close to You.

Getting to know You is unlike any other.
Loving You is the same as loving our mother.

Fix it Jesus, for You are the only One who knows *how*.
Teach us. Show us. Tell us *how* to change us in time *now*.

XXIII. I AM HE

The Father of Abraham, Isaac, and Jacob—
Nothing on Earth could or can't shake 'em!

Most definitely can't break 'em—
His creation, He did make 'em.

Destruction:
However,
Whatever,
Whenever,
Wherever,
Whichever, and
Whomever
life unfolds.

I am He, and He is within you!!!!!!!

At that day ye shall know that I am in my Father,
and ye in me, and I in you.
King James Version (John 14:20)

Printed in the United States
by Baker & Taylor Publisher Services